To the Dark Angels

Also by Jared Smith

The Collected Poems of Jared Smith: 1971-2011 (2011, NYQ Books)
Grassroots (2010, Wind Publications)
Looking Into The Machinery: Selected Longer Poems by Jared Smith
      (2010, Tamarack Editions)
The Graves Grow Bigger Between Generations
      (2008, Higganum Hill Books)
Where Images Become Imbued With Time (2007, Puddin'head Press)
Lake Michigan And Other Poems (2005, Puddin'head Press)
Walking The Perimeters of the Plate Glass Window Factory
      (2001, Birch Brook Press)
Keeping the Outlaw Alive (1988, Erie Street Press)
Dark Wing (1984, Charred Norton Publishing)
Song of the Blood: An Epic (1983, The Smith/Horizon Press)

To the Dark Angels

Jared Smith

NY
Q Books™

The New York Quarterly Foundation, Inc.
New York, New York

NYQ Books™ is an imprint of The New York Quarterly Foundation, Inc.

The New York Quarterly Foundation, Inc.
P. O. Box 2015
Old Chelsea Station
New York, NY 10113

www.nyq.org

Copyright © 2015 by Jared Smith

First Edition

Set in New Baskerville

Layout by Macaulay Glynn

Cover Photo by Jared Smith

Author Photo by Deborah P. Smith

Library of Congress Control Number: 2015931177

ISBN: 978-1-63045-003-8

To the Dark Angels

Acknowledgements

I want to thank the editors of the following e-zines, journals, and anthologies for first accepting the following poems:

After Hours: *"Voyagers"*
Big City Lit: *"Having Almost Forgotten Why I Was Here"* and *"Not Owning An Address"*
Heavy Bear: *"My Father's War Again"*
Home Planet News: *"Among so Many Opportunities"* and *"Einstein's Brain, Divvied up Now,"*
Ibbetson Street Review: *"Broadband Man"*
Manifest West Anthology, (Western Press Books): *"Front Range on Fire"*
The New York Quarterly: *"The Weather Maker"*
The Paterson Literary Review: *"When We Moved"*
The Pedestal Magazine: *"This Woman to The Dark Angels,"* and *"Prelude to a Drought"*
Poetry Bay: *"Equinox,"* *"Auden's Apartment,"* and *"What We Don't Talk Of"*
Reckless Writing Anthology, Vol 2, (Chatter House Press): *"I Don't Hang Out in Bars Anymore Either, of Course"* and *"Looking For Life on Mars"*
SOL: *"Pick to Shoulder Against Stone"*
The Same: *"A Most Important Day,"* *"As One, All,"* *"For Dinner Shared Their Meat,"* *"In Epiphany,"* and *"The Professor's Den"*
Spillway Magazine: *"Among The Early Discarded"*
Token Entry: New York City Subway Poems (Smalls Press): *"Briefly Back to The City"*
Turtle Island Quarterly: *"Alien in The Beasts of Burden"* and *"Lake Peterson"*
Wilderness House Review: *"After Our Argument,"* *"Bobolink Trail,"* *"I've Only Started to Become Aware,"* *"In Walls of Wood and Stone,"* *"Moments of Poets I Remember,"* *"Today so Cold Each House,"* *"Two Ends of a Shoelace,"* and *"Shivering Between Beings"*

Contents

for Deborah Parriott

"It is true, he said, "that they live in a machine—the city itself. But if the machine can emerge from nature then, surely, nature can emerge from the machine"

—Mark Helprin

Shivering Between Beings

What we build endures
  from the fleet hoofed animals
    grained grasses
      spaces between stars
endures beyond understanding
  white within darkness
in the primeval without words

There is a web between
  what we build and the ephemeral
    tight as a seine net
      as sanity itself
it is woven from the waters
and all nourishment they carry
in silicate-like chains of sediment
unknown to our minds or thought

Beneath this thin parchment
  cover of impermanence
    eggshell white
      fragile,
endures beyond the hands and words
this framework a city of broken fingers
parched breastbones dried pelvic thrust
endures a meaning outlasting flesh
whistled down alleyways

                    II

Does something speak in the grasses
  sifting sunlight
in an early autumn meadow?
Does a mountain stream soothe,
or air fill the fragrance of memory?
Does the silhouette of a woman

13

gazing sadly from an open window
unlock something not of bone or flesh?
Is the artist with her brush aware of color
finding a home within yourself?
Has not this always been?

There is nothing of matter.
A candle burns on a table
in a shadowed room.
There is no one present.
It burns in a pewter holder
   tinctured by time.
The shadows are its flame.
An open book lies on the table.
What we build endures.

III

The distillation of grasses
and the web woven the stones
the waters filled with sun
and the spaces between stars
becoming solid as bone
buried deep unseen within flesh
coming upon flesh
become bone filled with stars
and in this too the bone endures
from shape to shape and time to time
lost without memory of words.

It takes a long time to break into the sacred
   from the grasses
     though they are filled with sun,
       as are the arches of an abandoned barn
gone to weather where men once worked

where shadows play across spider webs
where horses have wandered from their stalls
long ago and the air is heavy with mold
and words spoken to men and beasts are dust
and what endures is hardly known
though built of the transference of time.

A hawk rises from a neighbor's field
   turns sideways into wind
     catches the scent of flesh
bumps up against an unviable net
turns toward the sun dips down
screaming into wind that lifts it
finding spaces between the words
that are beyond its ability to speak.

And the flesh...
it shivers between beings.

The Early Storm

While we have been sleeping, the waters
of our reservoir, the waters of our fields,
the slow deep rivers of our profound sorrow,
the morning dew that escaped last May,
which climbed the clouds of autumn
has started to descend again as shavings,
as slivers of the moon that have touched stars.

They have nestled among blue spruce limbs
and among Douglas firs first, then juniper,
then between the outstretched fingers of pine,
filtering and nestling down then into nettles,
coated the deep blue Oregon grapes, red rose hips,
sage, tufts of grasses, coating the ice of waters
that they rose from, and rising again this time white
so that from the window now all trees are the same
and the grasses and the roads and buildings too
as what is white and what is shadowed grows
    to meet itself.

It takes at least a year of not thinking of these things
to see how they come together when the earth reaches up
and the first snows in their turn come down among stars
that have drifted from the time we too were among them,
and we reach up and trees and seeds and everything we see
becomes itself as one. We are standing by the window
thinking something happens while we sleep, something
that unburdens us from what we think we are. We see
strange impressions, paw prints, in that first snow each year
where things misshapen somehow have come to explore our home,
sniffing around the cornices, the sidewalks, icy garden beds,
in the night while we sleep, and then drawing back again. I know
they too will be filled or stretched beyond their boundaries
by the time the sun is fully risen and the snow is fully flown.

What We Don't Talk Of

Our language is one forged from
fists slammed down on desks,
from Teutonic storage bins forged
from fire for cold steel weaponry.
It is a scaffolding for science
measured and contained too small;
a brittle thing matching the metal
that places fences in our pockets.

Our language does not understand
nor have words for sunrise coating
and enmeshing autumn grains
growing where water meets the land.
It does not understand the lightness
filling the dark between trees at night.
The wind moves between its words
as though they were but dried shells.

Our language but mimics the eyes
of fox stealing the eggs from chicks
or taking meat home for the pups.
Our syllables get caught in its fur
and brushed out by brambles
scattered to fleshless tangles of rage.
Our language is one of frustration,
unable and unwilling to be flexible,
unwilling to listen to the words
of welcome that come from your lips,
unwilling to forgive what it does not know.

Auden's Apartment

When he was at Swarthmore Wystan wrote
what he wanted most as a tow-headed boy
walking among the grains of Wales was
to prospect and excavate a lead mine,
perhaps knowing then of making men heavy
as the centers of their consciousness
where the wings of world wars would fail.
What a way for words would follow
as Achilles' heel would fail and fall
creating victories where armor rattled
around one and darkness veiled the eyes.

I hunt for the little things in poets.
How little we become of what we want.
How insubstantial in the weight of worlds
weighing down upon man's history.
Frost bitter cold upon the bonds of family
yet breaking down the fences that we know,
and Dickey pickled in a vat of Sheep child,
Warren something slow in the mind of a cow,
a glass jar growing in Tennessee, and a howl
Bly tucks firmly behind his Mexican serape.
We go for these things, we Americans.

We have no mythology beyond misanthropy
unless it is of the little man against the storm.

In the Farthest Sky

How sun triggers the green fuse
one fiber at a time back away from its roots
into ethereal fire that dries to ash
home to home across light years,
where light years have depth beyond time.

How sun triggers the entire chain of space
back upon itself, a star from within stars
fervent with alien life across time. How
many life forms rise up into that fire.
Each one, and how many stars fire the fuse
across whatever lies between them that
their dust the dust of nova nights blows
to green filaments across chance. How
many chances cross these infinite miles.

Perhaps we are one species, green fern
and the fox that lies down upon its fronds
the corona of its eyes lighting time
where we come upon it in the morning
then looking deeply into each other's eyes
stones scattered almost silent beneath our feet.

How sun carries this deepest of gazes beyond
enveloping our DNA, our souls, our fear
and our love in energy packets traveling dark
beyond beyond until they reflect in some
something, perhaps a microfilament lying idle
in the ash of what once was and what will be.

Einstein's Brain, Divvied up Now,

ponders walls it could not imagine,
and more slowly now as it sits
on a worn wood shelf in a stone building
beneath brightly luminescent lights
dimly aware it is not all there, has left
slides of parietal regions cut away.
Still processes proceed at slower speeds
outside the can where digital abstracts run
and time curves around to meet itself

is largely contained within two mason jars
and preserved in alcohol within a cider box,
divided into two hundred different sections
but is missing other slices mounted on slides…
and the jars are sliding too through a door
into time that leads them back to space
caught in the heavy mass of earth's matter
and are outside the jar holding it perhaps
and marking visual maps upon a paper
with a violin playing in the foreground,
and it is holding a cup of coffee, playing
its awareness of a sandwich formed of cow
which grazes forever across the universe

is still hunting for its eyeballs which are
stored in a safe deposit box in New York,
recalls it had a doctor named Zimmerman
and gets tangled up in blue with Bob Dylan,
living in a basement in Philadelphia
hospital in New York patent office in Germany
computer technology on its way across space
beyond the outer fringes of our solar system
never quite finding itself speeding back upon it
or simply without the senses needed for man
to follow the path or speed of light

is alive at the same
time that it is dead,
and sits with William Burroughs
drinking beer beneath a cooler
in Missouri with Dr. Harvey,
then driving across America
in a Buick Skylark, and then
back to the pathology lab
at Princeton where he once
    hung out
coming out and going back

is perplexed in its oblong path
like a comet of gaseous matter
lighting stars that no one sees,
has great trouble finding words,
knows that after coming together
from the cosmos there is separation
which cannot speak across time
and space begins with time again

When We Moved

Ten years the homestead was abandoned,
or longer, I suspect, that being when we moved in,
and I suppose I should have walked in earlier
just to see why it was abandoned in that hollow
snug into the side of the mountain meadow
looking for all the world like a schoolmarm's home
with the remains of that white picket fence
and the rose bushes still blooming by the door,
but I always felt like someone else was watching,
might step up behind me when I cleared the door
and anyway it always looked like someone would
come home again today if not tomorrow, so, well,
it wasn't until last week that I went in, stepped
over the broken shards of glass, shone my light
into corners, finally descended the basement stairs,
and even then didn't come across anything at first
of course, but I can tell you I'm not going back again,
not even when the last boards begin to fall away.
There are some things you don't call the sheriff about
when you're trying to keep the land the way it was,
like I told you ten years ago when we moved in.

The Professor's Den

After the fire you wouldn't have known
if he hadn't labeled each one of them
what was in that collection he owned at home.
Just the shattered glass beneath the beams,
some scraps of paper scorched black, and bone
that could have been a bird collection, or one
of mice like those he kept at the university
where his students spent their post grad years.
But he wrote it down in his own hand, how
each small box contained one finger bone,
and each city he taught in had one box,
though all together now they were as one,
scattered across his library floor with the books,
their covers closed and gone, the floor itself
little more than a hole in time.

This Woman to the Dark Angels

The woman who last lived in my house
receives postcards from the institutions,
advising her what to buy and what to wear
now that the dead are lost in our computers.
What will make her bone shiny smooth,
her teeth white as the day they left behind.
Notices for art events in museum mirrors,
orchestras she no longer needs to listen to.
I hold piles of these notices in my hands.

No one to tell anymore that her name is Gone.
No way to tell the salesmen that she won't buy
under any conditions anymore.
Why don't her pension or social security checks
come in among the slicker stuff. I could use it.
But somehow the government seems to know,
not care but know…this beast that spies on
small gray ladies wandering deserted streets
without ever saying anything that it finds,
leaving each institution to do its own thing
and sell to the dark angels whatever it can sell.

Looking for Life on Mars

Spotting it will only enhance its camouflage,
but there are certain attributes that will define it.
It tries to make itself look pretty but not like a sunset.
Immortal, but not like a stone.
It likes to clean itself and multiply among like,
moving rapidly from one place to another
much like sand grains meeting the River Styx
but with the intention of coming back for more.
It most likely has a social structure
but does not spend time in front of a computer.
Has eyes that filter red sunlight at night.
Drinks water as if it were the driest of dust.
Is small on a planetary scale but large cosmologically.
Stands out sharply from its stark surroundings
like a digit on a disc in a distant cloud universe.
Gives off noxious gases when no one is looking.
Hides from things that burn holes in the ground.
It is likely to be as hungry as the wind.

Among so Many Opportunities

The girl expressionless in her chair as you read
in the back of the café is languorous
blonde and has led relief efforts
against AIDS in South Africa. She
stretches catching something in your voice.
She has tended inns with older men
danced with the dark woodland sprites
on the coast of Connemara. There are 12
in the room this evening you don't know
her but she draws the light from each corner,
has taught ESL in NYC ethnic neighborhoods,
tells you later she teaches dance
in alpine meadows next to alpine lakes
and that dance becomes space between words
and is paid to dance thusly by men outside
the system and parents of children who
turn away from the institutional doctrines.
But you don't know that, lost in your armor
talking to the suburban academic vacancies
you see in almost every college town café.

In That Three Miracles at Least

I am walking the high mountains
between Sacramento and San Francisco in winter
where it is dry and arid and snow is falling about me
swirling through my open shirt collar on that country road
no lights before me on either side, and no homes, no shelter
except the hobo songs I had taken into my heart as a boy
and yet there were stars above me and I took my heat from them
stars lend me your heat I say and keep walking
and a train calls to me from somewhere in the distance
a shadow passing between me and the mountains
and at last there came a fork between two dirt roads
and at that fork appears an all-night restaurant lights on
and I make it there so cold and sleepy I walk
straight to the front counter and say I have no money
and am cold and can you give me just a cup of coffee
and cradle it as life in my hands and walk to the back wall
with life in my hands with nowhere to go and no one wanting me
when a young blonde walks in to buy cigarettes and I
so unlike I am really
walk up to her and ask if she is going to San Francisco
and she says yes and I ask if I might get a ride and she looks down says yes
and that was two miracles that happened that kept me alive
that night and so she drives two hundred miles what were the chances
with me to a small graveyard just outside San Francisco
where she stops the car and we get out and visit
the grave of her husband who has just been killed in Vietnam
and I walk from there down into the city where I stay
sleeping on park benches during the day and in restrooms at night.
It was a bad time with little or nothing to eat but
I lived the hunger that kept me moving
after that. And in this I become or I became.

Apartment 62

I was summoned to be there
at that house, that time, that day, that said
the wild roses growing along the tracks
held an aroma that stopped all thought.
Pigeons waddled backward eyes cocked
first one way and then another bright
as the metal in a young girl's mouth.

Legs have a way of doing that
dot dance across years even in sleep,
a familiar song began playing in my shirt.
A man without a face calling into time
grabbed my hat and stuffed it in my trousers.
He was drowned out in the profusion of life
but his words were bullets entering unseen.

Streets of Macadam and of Cobblestone

The people not teaching idea to word to music
are also waking in the night hearing distant notes,
are also setting the kettle to heat upon the stove, singing
too to let the pain swell up from their hearts and out
into those spaces which are not bound by flesh.

Those who have not heard of nor read Chaucer
are those written of in the Canterbury Tales,
their dances and custom that of their lives,
and the songs they sing too unbound by flesh,
letting dreams swell up from hearts and out.

The people who are sweeping floors at night
sweep dust jackets of words along the boards
scratching soft reeds across varnished woods.
The butchers of hogs and cows chopping hard
too, are percussionists of simple notes repetitive.

The taxi driver opens his doors without pension,
learning to speak the languages of strangers,
carrying ideas from one set of doors to the next
in sweaty suits and perfumed evening gowns,
playing staccato back-thrust to engines exhaust.

This is the unpaid job of poets in their books
or in their rooms with students or without, with
lecture halls or coffee shops, the speaking
that comes from the unseen patterns of their days
and the echoes that come back from clothes,
the fabric of idea and the hollow flute of bone
played across deserted streets that end as they go on.

Not Owning an Address

Sitting in sun on the bench
he hears hints of expectations
what year is it now what
phone number rings in the night
what day of the week and where
do you live. Yes
thank you, I do
but in all the weight of years
the wait of time woven around ears
each infinite digit of each number
is a still point encompassing nothing
smaller or larger than the corona
of an eye and I'd as soon sleep
here in the heart of man
as any hard point in time.

I've Only Started to Become Aware

other people use our apartment at night.
They try to be considerate, inconspicuous,
gone before I am aware of them, but I know.
The coat closet hanging open when I wake,
tell-tale scratches on the coffee table,
a scrap of paper with indecipherable notes,
the number of wine bottles in the trash.

Someone called yesterday morning, and I
picked up the phone and answered, but it
was for another woman. The man insistent
at the end of a long tunnel of static corridors,
finally reciting our number twice, demanding
she call back, and then late that night came
banging on our door before I went to bed
and certainly before anyone else came in.

It's gotten so we don't have friends over,
because I can't keep the refrigerator filled,
or someone left a moldy tray of cheeses,
or the wood around the door is splintered.
It doesn't matter. These are little things,
but I don't like strangers coming in on us
or sitting behind the mirrors looking out.
I don't like the extra laundry in the hamper
or the dirty dishes in the sink when I get up.

Voyagers

Thirty-five years ago a linguist in academe
who was my father worked on symbols and sounds
imprinted on a gold disc to be contained within a
Voyager now entering the interstellar medium
attached to a most expensive tin can shot aloft.

Do not think of the unimaginable miles
or the dust or the water droplets or solar flares
growing more distant on the horizon of memory.
Maybe for just a bit, the blue birthstone
that was the beginning of so much measurement.

Or think of nothing at all imprinted on the hands
of men sitting around a campfire singing songs
celebrating the harvest that clings to their skin.
Think of the invisibility of miles on men's lips
and of the grooves time imprints on their minds.

We are at a parallel universe within ourselves.
With all this time and space, there are no cell
phones or internet connections connecting us
and the tin can contains time outside our own
fashioned from yearnings that grew to words.

A murmuring blows across these stars at night.
Our fine-tuned eyes turned up cannot hear the song.

Insomniac

A rusty barbed wire
left sagging from rotted posts
winds among yellow wildflowers
concentrating radio wave frequencies
as an antenna through earth across infinity.
Carl Sagan's voice Hitler's the signature
of helium atoms a strip of wire
across flowers picked last fall
here and I'm lying in bed again
dark in a cabin where each cell
in my body is oblivious padded walls
to the strings of Einstein's violin
night after night dealt to their trembling
slowing exhausting across generations
each cell's call back across the years
wars Hiroshima unpaid bills
undelivered paychecks of redundancy
these meaning so much to flesh
unbequeathed unmeant to vibrate
to these frequencies yet still I am.

Equinox

A grasshopper crawls over the twisted steel rail, rusting
within a hand's reach from where I sag down on haunches,
tumbles on its head, flails its feet on the rotting wooden ties
and takes to air tick-wickering the way grasshoppers do.
My fingers reach out to the yellowed aspen leaves,
testing their resilience which is not much, then dust.
I don't know why I have come to the end of this rail
way track that lies abandoned behind houses and rocks.
The sky has never looked so blue or the sun so dappled,
and my lungs are filled with the first cold air of autumn
from deep down where the wildflowers hold their roots.
Oregon grapes grow bitter but big in blueberry memories,
their thorny leaves strung in holly garlands along the ground.

The world ticks again, whickers, and wings fill the sunlight,
across our alpine meadow. The suits hanging in my closet
have so filled with time that they do not fit any longer. There
are dark men standing in the midst of forests all across our land.
They have their calloused hands out, calling silently.

Laying my hands to the steel bent and rusted, narrowing
toward home I feel still the hard hands of men who made this rail
a way of transitioning things that bring change from cities; those
hands torn lifeless now but not so long ago holding wars in Europe
between plantings of the seeds that grow around us now, and I
hear the winds of winter gather above our peaks, whipping
down wind and water carved canyons and through the aspen.
The mountains groan along that line of time, and space is
the opening of time between each leaf upon each trembling limb.

Each blade of grass, each leaf of sedge is sharp to the fingers,
cutting away the seasons of growth that gave it green,
each slender stalk tinged toward tomorrow with yellows,
browns, reds intertwined. And the air is bright with the
scent of an old lady's Depression era spice cabinet.

In the dark pools, the hidden riffles far above Boulder
in the off-road unmapped Indian Peaks Wilderness, the
sun is rising inside brown trout and smoking inside their sides
with all the colors of the mountainsides where no one sees.

They bend into the rocks themselves spending their spawn
into the fussilade of color that gives life to time, flesh to flesh,
encasing themselves in bright red eggs that are the dawn of everything
dark beneath the water that feeds upon the songs of crickets,
and I wonder what this rail is still doing here, scarring
this seam of land. I think at times I know.

My Father's War, Again

Germans knew everything about change,
and nothing about things that didn't change.
One year they liquefied a season's potato crop
for oil to run their trucks and tanks. Perfect
scientists, they ground lenses for high altitude
surveillance, froze farmers in their fields like
our satellites, magnified the shadows defining
each of us, learning to motivate machinery, cash
in on what it was to be defeated, to be a small
country recovering from being crushed, and we
took to that like rats, being back-home boys
ourselves growing grain while empires fell.

It takes a while to see this, a few years, I guess.
We've tried since to measure it in our businesses
and seize military efficiencies to meet our needs.
But I live in what was a farmhouse before the war.
Searching photographs from before I was born,
I see the church tower still standing on Main Street Square
and that Pete's Warehouse was once the depot where
trains carried green container cans one day and grain
the next and grain inside the green cans another day.

And the people, looking up from under wing-tipped collars,
staring forever into the camera's lens of measurement;
their own lens of the eye, the cornea, the hole into the soul
opening into the black tunnel that comes back upon itself.
It's other things than static measurement that make us men,
they seem to say, and there are times that do not change.

Pick to Shoulder Against Stone

Three nights and days an unusual October fog
has hidden the mountains, obscuring our
suburban park and the farm field beyond with
its whickering invisible and heavy-scented horses.
Still, after a day or ten it starts to wear, and
we wonder why we worked so hard to
come to this kitchen table in this room
where everything is gray but the marmalade
you spread on English muffins and the
shredded wheat I pour hot water on into a bowl.
The bowl is filled with violet blue glaze
and the wheat with stored autumn sunlight.
The marmalade remembers pelicans at dawn
as it finds its way down their long gullets.
There will be meetings to attend to today.
I string metal disks to my fishing lines and cast,
float steel feathers with talons into the wind,
knowing there is something out there I can't see
that sees you and me within its hungry dreams.
It is more than I can imagine gathering all that grain
and baking down dry dense pigments from the earth
generation after generation to a kitchen table
where we might sit drinking coffee on such days
when nothing outside is obvious and voices voices
that mean echoes across empty fields of gray.
Someone though has sat here for us, thinking
even as we push the handle of the toaster down
and things grow warm inside the box. Warmth
itself lights up little spaces across such dioramas,
heats our bellies and our eyes if we press them not
                too close.
When the sun comes out again we'll have to rise.
Surely the Chinooks will shake our bones again,
and the miners under our feet will begin their tread,
pick to shoulder against stone within the earth.
Hand-tooled metal wheels will begin to spin, dig

their way beneath the cities we have built upon our past
and the fog will lift again, but it won't be today
and we won't be sitting here thinking of this while
        it is going on
we are a complex mesh of flesh and what is in the mind.

Two Ends of a Shoe Lace

come apart every time Timmy plays dodge ball,
and they trip him up, causing him to leave his flesh
scraped on concrete. He associates pain and play.
His mother tries to stop him on the way outside
by saying your shoes are coming untied. They flap.
They will get caught under your soul. Again and again,
growing more flayed and thinner, dirtier, day by day.

He remembers this and ties polished Oxfords tighter going
off to his office where he slides among slick papers, but
they still untie beneath the fabric of his dark blue suits,
slapping against marble bank floors or wicking water
from the slush filled streets he dodges among. His hands
before meetings begin to be stained with mud from fields
he has crossed in coming here. He dreams of animals
that inhabit those fields and hide from computer screens.

But he ties the shoes tighter anyway. He double knots
loose ends that fly loose to lift him from his tracks.
He keeps his poise at last although it finally may come to loafers
with which he can't run as fast but at least can hold his own
ground with, gain his mental and physical poise and pose
the same way his polished desk does, his swivel office chair,
leaving little indication of the lives left changed at his hand.

Growing more important, he slips his evening slippers on and thinks
of the two ends of shoe laces and mother from those winter days.
There are so many loose laces of untied shoes sitting on shelves
with their tongues lolling out, stitching their eyes together, their
souls flat, black, ridged, well-heeled, tied together with each other.
He can't believe that after all these years he still comes untied so
easily whenever he is thinking of something else. And thus
he thinks that two and two are one at loose ends, and he is right,
but soon walks bare-footed where men can never talk again.

Artemidorus on Art and Dreams

When the majority of people in a democracy
are trained to care for their own house, wear more
than the lives of their neighbors; when their
children are taught sports on steroids in school,
when the seeds of semen are seen as more sacred
than men or the forests from which we build our societies,
then it becomes easy to divine the meaning of dream.
Each symbol has one meaning from one experience.
Each nerve set measured in each brain by sensors
lights up one meaning in any courtroom's logic,
and terrorists and sexual deviants wear red letters
on their breasts. Then, politicians become emperors
and render unto the dusty streets of the capitol that
which should be rendered not to gods but unto equals.
These are not prophecies nor editorials. I am but Art.

I am a young man two thousand years before Christ.
I walk along streets among mansions of the rich, and
stirring with my shoe laces the dust of the desperate.
Those who laid pipelines to bring us water from the hills
have been put to pasture in the seats of our Coliseum.
They wave their hands and cheer. We wave our swords.
Paint chips off so slowly when the wind blows that
we are not aware of the mist we live within. The shapes
and shades which flicker across windows in the night
are either one thing or another, and we weed them out
by what we carry in our minds outside the tinted walls.

This nail, glinting where it has fallen, is twisted and bent,
its head smashed in attempting to hold something together
where it lies in the middle of the road. But nothing holds.
Perhaps we have a piece of parchment ripped from meaning,
perhaps we have the line where two doorways met and came
apart one last time, perhaps it held a knocker up
to bring someone to the door; or perhaps a cart to carry more
nails across the country to put things right the way they were:

these are the things diviners see, meaning many things in one
surrounded both by what they have and what they were and
what the heck, it is a noble business to see these things
and state them. Men will make of them what they will.

The Weather Maker

To become aware of the eyes that watch you from mountains,
the presence that is aware of you when it is evening and rocks
themselves have faded into shadow beyond silence, to become
at ease with the waters of mountain streams, you have first to be
aware that there is nothing as big as this vast Weather Maker. Nothing.
you have seen or will ever see, and nothing
that one can wrap words around or linear thought around.
Not even this Weather Maker itself, which is silent but jingles deep
in your pockets with your change while walking New York streets.
This weather maker which fills the bottles of Wyoming bar rooms
blows across the Great Sand Dunes of Nebraska, rattles
windshields of heavy trucks, derails tanker trains, buries
everything in its path becoming a part of them. There is nothing
there in our little time in our little place beneath a pure blue sky
where peaks spill in slow tectonic motion eastward higher than
all the towers built by civilizations across time sleepless still
in a realm where man has never sought to build or do business,
this engine yet drives the dynamo that built the cities at its base,
and it is nothing but stone when you try to say what can be seen.

> Just sit here by the fire with hobo guitar harmonica
> playing along the cadence of rain and wind
> singing to your lover with words that do not mean
> a thing beyond crickets and the scent of sage,
> bringing peace to the silence surpassing all.

It's true today you can put a GPS on any part of the earth, pinpointing
each promontory by satellite, or can walk down old jeep roads
leading from one abandoned mine to another or one lake to another
across the barren ground lying between each. But you cannot mark
out the barren ground, for it is barren and in that there is growth.
There are books and notes on ecological shifts taken in log cabins
sitting in one clearing or another hidden by the trees, notes which
will drive commodity prices in New York and politics in Washington.
There are veins of gold and silver and kimberlite and uranium
and coal and talc and garnets and jade that are squeezing up caught

within tectonic time and plates, spilling out here in the Weather Maker,
rolling eastward while rolling up the wealth of a continent
and spilling it across the sere dry heartland which we farm so hard.
The words are hard to understand, and hard to find, and hard to say.
This is what watches us and is aware of us and what we want to be
in the middle of change in the middle of our lives in the middle of time.
It all comes down to this. There is nothing like it anywhere that we can say.

> Sit down among these Rocky Mountains,
> and their foothills are but a trough in the waves of time.
> They are filled with the blank white eyes of steers
> heading to rodeo, and the yellow glint of cougars.
> They are filled with the songs of cowboys who have gone home
> and corral gates waiting forever to be closed.
> They are filled with the migrations of mighty animals
> here in the 21st century, of elk and moose and bear.
> The streams with trout bright as the berries growing upon their banks.

Filtering now past The Gold Act and The Silver Act of 1893,
when Colorado produced 60% of U.S. silver and then next to nothing,
and men walked from the empty pits of their mines for the last time leaving
the earth empty of their sweat but still filled with stone that would remember
the rotting timbers that they left behind and the empty wail of wind along
long deep corridors that exited and entered again into time. Let's get past
the ornamentation and past the world trade built on that metal to dominate,
and past the World Wars and the armies whose metal and bombs were built
here in the Weather Maker beneath the storms that fly east across New Mexico
whipping around the hogans of Native Americans and the town plazas,
spreading sleet along the well-lit highways and ending lives in ice.

This thing comes with you and its molten core churned from the earth
in the rotation of the sun and its magnetic poles between its parts.
The bones, the heavy metals, and the star dust and life across the cosmos.
They're here, sure they're here, but you can't imagine how to spell them out.
You take words and think about them, and the words are concrete constructions
out of which we built the Periodic Table of all the elements we live by.

43

You take a snapshot, maybe. There's Oppenheimer on his ranch riding the hills.
There's Rocky Flats and the dead men walking with cancer in their lungs.
The Atomic Age. The meth labs in little tin trailers at the edge of town.
The sage growing up into the sand dunes and the water draining out below.
The molly-be-damned molybdenum mines that hardened our metals.
There's little left without it. Without the rain the Weather Maker forms
which sweeps the air clear each day across America and feeds the grains.
What we do with it is what we do. That's all. It's always churning up,
reforming, rolling beneath our feet and rising above our clouds. What
we do with it is what we do. And there is nothing as big as it has always been.

Front Range on Fire

The mountains are coming on us,
are filling the lungs,
they are retreating from stone
heavy as ghost flesh, wispy
lives choking out life everywhere.

A woman sitting beneath a pinon tree
feels wind separate strands of her hair
until her scalp itches, moves her
gray skirt over snow white thigh, passing
over her nipples in their cashmere nest,
warm globes and without words reaches
into her purse, her long delicate boned fingers
feeling for anything lost in the smoke within.

How many fires light the front range states?
I am talking of the fire within you
that fills books and musical interludes
swirling upward and outward forever,
and I am talking of the fire outside you
that rages in the empty beds of your house
and all the houses along your ridge,
and I am speaking of the fire outside
that is breathed into your lungs from pine
and exploded homes of cedar whose walls
now contain the immensity of what is beyond,
how many fires that the media reports
and how many others they fear to dream of?
How many keys empty of their locks?

For Dinner Shared Their Meat

At the deepest depth
of the darkest alpine lakes
where blood cells crystallize
lake trout dwell, their bellies
hungry for the darkness of stars
where it is winter in the soul.

But this evening when I walked to the inlet
they were there invisible beneath the waves
an easy cast where they were never before
and some voice told me to tie on a heavy lure,
a Mepps golden spinner #5 from France
and cast it into the turbulence
of mountains meeting reservoirs
and bang one and then another
of these dark messengers, and
once again you were not there
to see this little thing this time unspool
in ways that had never happened before,
and I was only a man with a thin coat
standing out there against the wind,
so I battled and unhooked them
brought their dark sunsets home with me
for dinner, shared their meat
into the meaning of it all
of what it means to be human.

Bobolink Trail

Bobolinks were blown along Boulder Creek
again last week like the year before about this time,
their black white feathers wound about each twig
each gold capped head enamored of the sun
twisting about and capping each green clipped leaf
going golden and themselves between each branch
unable to be discerned between each temporary perch
being there and gone at once as the autumn wind.
So many thousands in a stream of feather shadows.

We sit in coffee shops and argue again the old
familiar testosterone saws about abortions, marriages,
who wears the pants and who takes them off of whom,
of missiles tending fields along the Yangtze—
another turn of the world from where we are but
knowing that the world is round we know it comes
again 364 times before the seasons complete their change
imprinted over each of us again and again in places
that can't be measured between space and time.

Lake Peterson

This is a small lake but deep,
nestled in the throat of a volcano
surrounded by miles of moose and elk
foraging their ways among aspen and fir,
the chuckling of martens and porcupines,
the silence of Colorado coyotes at dusk.

A sunset brightening horizon fills this lake
as it fills the sleek bellies of trout down
    in their darkness
with eyes that perceive what cannot be
    spoken,
what cannot be shared across flesh.
And the wind which passes among pines
moves across this lake without moving it,
meaning that small waves dance in place
where shore meets land again and again,
almost as on the edge of the Atlantic Ocean
except there are fewer people here
and there are no billboards, no road.

This is a small lake that matters little
where an eco-system of life encompasses
little meaning on the edge of infinity,
and the sun is its reflected surface
and its voiceless denizens are dark
with the bright colors of stars on their skin,
and the voice and temperature of the earth
funneled deep into its concave infinite depth.

Because the Animals Lust

we take them into our hearts
when they look not to our fields for food,
and we learn to care for their offal
and gather the grains of flesh that feed them
harboring them from death until their time.

There is little planning. They take
what is theirs to take not with concentration
not with lust but with luck of the draw
on little paws that follow our absurdities
or stealthy flesh eating sinews of the night,
but we take them into our hearts.

We take them into our hearts
because they too have survived the flood
that surpasseth all their understanding
and raise their young wherever life allows,
looking out of cold hurt eyes upon the land
they have formed umbilical bonds with
across time that words cannot breach.

Because we carry so many within our flesh
building upon what they have seen and believed
without having ourselves to understand we take
them into our hearts even as children,
holding their warm hairy sides against us and
looking into their wide and calculating eyes.

In Walls of Wood and Stone

The walls of my house stone
sculpted by glaciers many millennia ago
and swept by the sweat of imprisoned men
tumbled down mountain creeks
in the freshet spring rains
enforced by mighty trees whose limbs
are of the eternal burrowing into earth
rooting slowly among the grubs and fast life
until their mighty limbs grew heavy dead gold
and were lopped off, polished thin and set
as framework that would withstand insurance
speculators and investors of Wall Street drugs.
The carpet crème de la crème of polyphenes
woven across stark wallboard barbecue.
A home to last a lifetime in ghettos of the soul,
so we parse it out having paid our tithes.
Take off the carpeting, refinish the floors,
buy rock sculptures to hang upon the walls,
run wires vibrant with the world wide web
through the stones that grew eons ago
upraised upon a continent not yet discovered,
enlisting lighting, nuclear power, the dark of coal
to carry meaning among men and place it here
where I, my wife, and daughter sleep at night
and our dogs run pale from room to room
shadows in the darkness beneath a setting moon.

A Murmur in the Background

There is a murmur in the background,
disguising itself in wind on grass or trees,
in grains of sand rolling across granite,
in the LCDs lighting up men's wrists,
the ocean coming in upon itself in time,
the cells of your soul sloughing off as skin.

Unexpected Things

It's the unexpected things happening to your body
late at night that mumble in their sleep about age.
The sudden mole that appears above your eyebrow,
the salamander suddenly crawling across your collar bone,
the walrus concealed beneath your heavy gut.
Nothing wrong or obscene about these things.

Prelude to a Drought

Spring rains led to death beneath
a sun so hot the skies went dark.
I trailed elk across our meadow
snapping off each blade of grass
like slivers of wood in August.
Berries dried still green on bushes
and bears began to prowl our yard.
A dry wind found its way inside
and the mirrors darkened as
dawn gave way to evening gowns
and empty hangers dangling in closets.

Report From the Fire Division

In 2012, forest and brush fires scorched 384,803 acres in the state, destroyed 650 homes and killed six people, according to the Colorado Division of Fire Prevention and Control.

Is there any wonder big cities fear the greenbelt or its bindings in the mountains of the soul, and lay concrete thick and heavy about their feet.

Something green *is* growing in the cities now, though it is dark, laden with smoke, but it is carried in the deep pockets of their citizens and it is dark.

Coyotes having haunted the burned out habitats of mountains are following the greenbelts, are abandoning them to the shadows cast by the harvest moon and moving in.

But there is less acreage to build concrete upon each year, less lineage to the earth when there is less land for grass and coyote and yucca and man.

Cut back the trees and send more water to the cities,
and bury their feet in concrete as you drop them off my boys.

As One, All

As one, all butterfly thin
leaves of aspen emerge at night,
this nutrient gathering tree grubbing
minerals from the earth where
tendril roots connect mountainsides
beneath the ground one organism
beneath the earth featuring thousands
of mouths thousands of full-throated trunks
emerging as one each year to sun
but only at night, dark on dark
their green filigree to emerge at dawn
filling their limbs with butterflies
and the iridescent shrill of hummingbirds.

How do these root vegetarians
connect their wits and timing for the sun,
bringing themselves together each year
in their fecundity between heaven and hell
atop the alpine meadows drawn
from midnight to sun each year
as we sleep in our hardwood cabins?

The Neighborhood News

Jean got stuck in the toilet at the Gas 'n Go
the day her husband was laid
off his job and shot his old flame in Detroit
just fifteen months back from Afghanistan,
and that led to child services taking her son
when she failed a DUI on the way to her mother's.
It's a story you don't hear on the nightly news.

Ed tagged down a car on Interstate 94
the night his sister passed away from cancer.
He met his quota that night while she died
smiling into a blank white hospital corridor
with something in her mind that had no words.
At what point do the drugs come home
with therapeutic value outside of money?

Bob, a set of nails set upright on the highway.
Tom, an argument with his father before departing.
Susan and Cheryl sharing a whispered secret.
At what point do the drugs come home.
It's a story you don't hear on the nightly news,
but at least the neighborhood spokesmen are talking
on tv. with presidential candidate spokesmen,
and it's well and the sports are on top and the weather,
well, too, the weather with Jimmy Cantrell is swell too
and the storms will pass far from the neighborhood news.

In the Cinema

We mistake electricity for men.
How little we know of ourselves.
Our empathy filled with shadows.

Among the Early Discarded

I rise before it is time,
and encounter my ghost rattling
between the minute hands of clocks.
No coffee on the burner, no light in the windows.
Our neighbors have no names anymore.
We are living in a sleek seed pod wind-whipped
igniting whatever place we come to land.
We have a ferocity beyond tooth and claw
which has been encased in paper products
but now when the lights are not working
I can hear the turning of wheels hidden
in the darkness before birth.

Each tooth of each wheel clicks into place.

It Seems Enough Almost

It seemed enough to mow the lawn,
to tend the morning glories, pull the weeds,
plant a few tomatoes and rows of peas
when spring blew off the western slopes
setting the elk to browsing, beavers to dam,
rivers to cascading over bone dry banks.
That's all…just to finish filling out the bills,
drive home and tend those things that waited
no matter how impatiently they grew
while the sun shone and the world whirled
and the drone of computers filled our days.

It seemed enough to collect the paycheck,
to carry it around and turn it to other things,
to get from the mountain range's western slope
 to east in half the time it took the waters
 to flow from there to here, and then go back,
 wondering what could one pick up in half the time
that waters wore away each grain of sand upon the land,
tasting of the ancient horror/honor of universe
while automated drones and droning filled our days.

Enough now, I think, to pluck a rounded stone
and send it skimming from my calloused hand
now that all of that has been left behind in time,
and walk where I can watch the waves go out
concentric circles from that shallow depth I saw.
A path I know now not ploughed in furrows
but circles in forests of time where no one walks alone.

In Epiphany

Seen in the snow last night
the dark creatures of your dreams
thrust their chests against each other, whistling
until the small birds of your hands answered,
unweaving the nests that kept them warm
and offering the bright globes of their future
to whatever wind would have them.

All across the Front Range
men dropped their pencils and ran
to warm their windows with the eyes of time.
Fire was urged from the darkness of logs
that lay buried in living rooms,
but something larger and darker than these,
something wild with the seeds of shadow

loped backward across the whitened fields,
something maternal with wind in its mane.

Today so Cold Each House in the Valley

Today so cold each house in the valley
is sending plumes of smoke into the air,
pushing its way across the razor's edge
of virtual reality, hazing into distance.
No animal tracks fleck the fresh snow.
Yet life moves even so at twenty below.

You are sitting downstairs at the T.V.
and I am in my study on the computer.
The dogs are sleeping or played out,
our daughter at the movies with friends.
Temperature going to five below.
If no one answers ads, ads are meaningless.

A Poet, His Wife, and Words

Repeatedly I try to read to her
the words of distant friends,
their music being the tone of love,
but she is busy in the hall of noise…
the egg whisk missing, muttering
under breath, turning on heel,
mixing cornmeal pancakes on the
iron grill on the old pot stove
in this cabin hewed from logs,
clattering utensils at me.
She hears every word I say
and at times can quote them back
but not from the silence. No,
from the catering and caring.
My words and those of friends
fall cold and glowing as aspen
into the cold of October winds.
At last I rise and grabbing saw
with bent teeth cut a cord of wood.

After Our Argument

After our argument I drive alone
up canyon into stone mountains,
moon so bright I hardly need headlights
under temperatures well below freezing.
I stop outside Nederland above Barker,
walk to cliff edge and look out over ice—
every shade of gray and white without motion
and moonlight painting caves and indents.
In places a yellow room opens beneath ice
and people set their tables, turn up music,
roll back chairs, hold each other lightly,
brushing lips against what is illusory.

Up here I can see each stone clearly,
each dried weed stalk fallen against winter.
I empty my bladder among them,
fill my lungs with distant stars, climb
into my car and head on up mountain
to where our road diverges from blacktop.
Our house lies 23 miles east of here
where you warm leftovers on an open range.

It Is as Much the Dog

Watching dog alert head on paw
carefully laid fire three logs across
two over
and two women in the room.
I'm sitting silently. The women reading.
The other man is outside.
He is the bigger man with guitar.
The air smells of burning pine and aspen.
The air crackles.
Light consumes.
Heavy animals know to stay away from light:
They are fur coats of ideas.
The ideas come out of darkness.
The room is as large as three people
and a dog.

We are the embers of decayed stars
catching light from burning logs in our eyes.

Beyond Quantum Physics

If a woman slips and falls
on the floor and can't get up
and no one is around,
does she get up and dance
in one of the parallel universes?
Does time explode on her tongue?
Do fawns wander down from the meadows
and butterflies lift her key chain?

When Steve Jobs lay dying
he cried out Oh Wow three times
and then slipped beyond paperwork
into something greater than he imagined
somewhere within beyond.

Broadband Man

Broadband Man is striding toward me
stumbling over his own shoulders
and I rush to him tweeting to my friends
who get messages of pizza and lingerie.
IRT subways in the sixties with graffiti
with a girl so young it rains in Manhattan.
Channel surfing the ads without Tivo,
and the toothy commercials blaring bongs.
Click an alley with exploding men and cars
Click an Oscar on the news Egypt blowing up
as we talk Football in Denver 2013 Click
body odor and erectile dysfunction rife
everyone every single body in my place
Click red bull in front of the NRA sites.
damn your bong bong lips are sweet honey
hard as the virtual screen on my dream, love.
I am running down a long rain-drenched alley
learning the proper way to handle spreadsheets,
each door I pass a gangster in a trench-coat
with no time to figure out if it is me there
looking from my screen as the world runs by.

Just the texture of the times interwoven nebulae.
Nothing much to see…just move along, citizen.

Ode on an American Earning

The granting of mortality comes slowly
for those of us who work the wheel,
the actuality of death making us human
and closing the doors we have left hanging.
Poets have words for flesh unblemished,
but those words are slow developing slowly
gathered from each mistake we make,
our hands circled around the chase
to win what will be won. It takes raw youth
and time to work the patterns, shape clay
with colors carrying the patina of meaning,
a time that lingers between the workings
of grandfather clocks and cell phones,
accumulating in the dust of empty rooms.
No instant messages, no quick network
comes from this where time stands still,
just a slow communication that enfolds.

Alien in the Beasts of Burden

The people are singing
as they march off again to war.
They are feeling their hearts
thud against the cosmic dust
of their bones against night
pressed uniform rank on rank
comforting each other, lowing
alien in the beasts of burden.

The Feral Gardener

Before I hand you this tomato
you must understand its ugliness
is one of palette not of palate.
That it is filled with the tart acidity
of summer nights in suburbia.

Home-grown rather than institutionalized,
its contents expand beyond its splotched ochre skin
which is wrinkled and split by nature
even before reaching the ripeness of adolescence.

This tomato will deprive you of the enjoyment
which is found at commercial salad bars.

A Most Important Day

I stand outside the party
spectacles frosted by a bowtie
fingers running up your legs
we say all the right things
champagne catching in the thr-
oat little explosions of matter
cocktails brimming in our hands,
the digitals sound becoming image
wavelengths in trench coats.

Uniquely the Same

Each cow lay, its DNA displayed
between plastic and cold Styrofoam.
Genetic butterfly myth run amok.

Moments of Poets I Remember

Auden, hungry, scrabbling for a cigarette.
Robert Hazel eating a chicken egg at breakfast
  with the heart still beating within its yoke.
Corso sitting on the curb at the corner of Infinity
  crying because a girl from Missouri locked him out.
Ginsberg as caveman with slouch, a bag over shoulder
  containing copies of Howl and an American Express
 Card zip machine.
Packard smoking and twirling a pair of some girl's panties
  by one hand sitting by an overflowing garbage pail.
Merwin looking up with pen in hand, puzzled suddenly.
Robert Penn Warren's post card arriving, saying I
  feel low as a dog…have been visiting the Berbers
  and riding camels.
Galway Kinnell digging beneath a beach house on Cape Cod
  to winter over.
Bly gathering us in across an empty stage with his serape.
Wendell Berry warning a girl not to hang out with old men
 lest she get balled.
Winans in an armchair photographed with Bobby Kennedy.
Hundreds and hundreds and hundreds of others you know also
and the intensity encased in bottles and smoke and mirrors
outside the lecture halls and thank god the university reading circuits.

These are tiny envelopes of vast universes
I have seen and flung myself into the heart of trees to read;
and into the black ink of man's meanings when he is lost;
and they are sea shells that remind me he is always lost,
but that it is his recognition of the vastness of which he speaks
that has the power to draw others in to catch their breath.

Disturbances

I am the word
      in the space
            in the continuum
shaped by aspen leaves
upon a mountain meadow
flowing the alpine cascades,
the ohm not constricted
      by being open
but squeezed by elemental boulders
within what is within the wind.

I remember The Times reporting
Allen Ginsberg being beaten by thugs
back on those dog soiled Village streets of 68
and rolling in the street gutters being kicked
and singing ohm when they wanted money
ohm opening through the pain
ohm between the books
the opening between other letters
ohm across the years ignored
still by the minds of time
stilled by the toughened soles of time.

Iamintheohm
adisturbanceseekingidentity
iamwordbeyondfragranceofflesh
andmindallendownopenalleys
inpatternsimaginedwhenallisall
aretherenotmeaningfulreverberations
betweensinglelettersbetweenwords
wewouldfillin?

Back Briefly to the City

Coming in from Colorado now,
I find the IRT departing from a different corner
of the terminal and trains are quieter,
and the old Italian deli man isn't there with
his lines of lunchtime customers, but still
the building in the building goes on all the same,
and I walk outside to where my Park Ave office was
and looking up to the seventeenth floor of windows
find the building in my office building still goes on,
and that the building in that room affects me not at all.
I return to the tunneling rooms of lethargy in Grand Central,
and find my way again to the IRT downtown local,
get off at Astor Place and walk the windows of Washington
Square as well as the bookstore windows and university.
The Chock Full O' Nuts is filled with sandwiches now,
the dormitories stacked with new-bred sacks of flesh.
Poetry washes in the gutters around the lips of cigarettes.

I am tired now. This is where my poetry comes from,
or where the tools to set it loose were sharpened,
in these factories where women were chained to their desks
before I studied in the rooms where the Shirt Tail Waist Factory
fire broke out to set a nation's labor laws in motion; where
rooms are boxes in the boxes of the years we call our life,
and where we fashion containers to take across our continents;
empty spaces containing eyes and falsified memories, and
setting these empty spaces anywhere we want across our land.
I sleep in the rooms of old friends who have stayed in touch
and talk with them about mountains they will never see,
and about a moose that comes out of the evening every other night
and steals past my cabin, brushing against a wooden wind chime,
and about the effect all our drinks together have on him
while we talk about poetry and meaning and I try to wake myself
to rush outside and grab a plane and come back and tell you
you have to come here where pre-history fills your lungs at all times.

That's why I've come here now, it seems, but I'd like a drink first
and to choose among the many sleek women in their furs with
all the secrets of taxi cabs run out into the city night on sequined feet.

People Making of It What They Will

Gulls are turning over abandoned warehouses
down by the Hudson River waterfront. Pigeons
strut where longshoremen sweated, and otherwise
the city is disconnected from this former commerce.
But the sun rises and Morton Street does connect.
I turn my back on ghosts and shattered glass
balconies looking out over what we have done.
I turn my back upon the old whalers and their ships,
the garbage that was taken out at dawn for years,
and the condominiums built between their ribs,
walking northeast over concrete covered streams
toward taverns where the music plays and poets dream
and universities have raised their stone facades.

The piling of pallets upon grates
banging metal dropped by heavy gloves
never stops before darkness nor starts beyond dawn
in front of every cursing store along West 4th Street
boxes piled upon frames in front of brick boxes
each one swarmed by a handful of heavy men
calling out Hey Joe, Hey, watch it,
against the cold settling before pedestrians come in
and each box sealed so the store owners know but no one else
each store therefore largely ignorant of all its neighbors
and the dark tunnel trucks that come in in endless shifts
boxes themselves en route from boxes
where heavy metal was poured perhaps for smaller hands
shaping key or machine tool parts or rosaries
going on down elevator shafts into the darkness
beneath dimpled shutters that are stamped with wads of gum.

The people come for this every day
in every city where meat is eaten or clothes are worn
or goods are sent out in exchange for not so goods,
and the heavy men speak of them all the same
Hey Joe, how's your boy making out now

and where's he off to
and its beer and sweats and prom dresses too
or grains to feed the horses of the apocalypse
and cleaning supplies and beauty creams
stacked where the pigeons walk and dogs wet
and then taken away to be raised up behind glass cases for display.

What do you make of this all, I wonder,
at times. The excitement of a woman's legs
ascending also, or her hands reaching out, her eyes
her hair blowing in a mid-day morning breeze.

A metal band binds each box.
A metal magnetic band binds each wallet
lying within each pair of pants or pocketbook
snug among old Kleenex and perfume unwrapped gum
sticks car keys keys to penthouses and drives safe deposit
boxes upon boxes numbered in digital phenomena
slick as the stripe down the center of a highway out
each month until it stops or goes underground.

What is to be made of all these things that are made,
piled, interchanged, heaped on sidewalks, used
to measure the worth of those things that are not made
on sweatshop floors but in the moments of our passion?

Having Almost Forgotten Why I Was Here

I stand flat against window glass in Manhattan,
pressing my palm against the cold winter of evening.
The lights are out. The bellman rings and slips an envelope
under the door. The plastic in my pocket is fulfilled.
The closet is empty now, but for an unused bathrobe.
Shampoo bottles oddly bright with infused light by the bath.
My forehead leaves a smudge of DNA against the night,
and as moments pass I push my hips too against the glass.
With a luck of sorts I will fall into what surrounds me now
and my past will meet me in the eyes of a coyote pausing
on the moonlit night ice of Central Park with no entity.

And so to Home

A gust of snow curls along the pavement, glancing off my shoes.
They are cowhide polished to an inch of their lives. Their eyes shut
forever, but I watch for them and with the wind my eyes rise
over rooftops engaging the skyline of Manhattan. It is twenty years ago.
Each window holds the warmth of a woman I have never met,
and each of them is folding undergarments away in cedar chests.

The snow is dry and light. It swirls up about my coat, and fills my hair.
I spread my arms and drop the spreadsheets that encase me.
While nobody is watching from urine soaked alleyways I turn my eyes
more directly overhead, squinting sideways to the universe and ride
the glass beads of pavement upward, shimmering between the clouds
of fossil fuels that fire our ways and escape into the spaces that lie immense
between our constellations, always there and the same as those that lie high
above Spencer Mountain to the west. There are senses we are aware
of that are infinite.

And Shadows in the Room

When I go, it's likely I will have had too much to drink.
I have mixed my sunsets and my grains as medicines, and
have reveled in the profound intoxication of the mind like
Davies or Coleridge or Wordsworth. Scientist and poet poet.
but I drink to you, all over the floor sometimes or more nobly
and to the generations we have overlapped or lapsed.

Tonight I pulled my grandfather's schedule for the Cambridge
street cars he took from his home each morning to his parish hall
and home again from where he left it tucked inside his copy of
Matthew Arnold with side-notes about what had happened to Mildred,
she of the hidden last name who needed words of hope in prayers
hidden tucked between the pages of books moved to my library
fifteen times across the years and across this country while I grew.
I don't know what made me open it up tonight, or why I did not
find it in my years of walking Washington or financing the dead,
but there it is, his DNA in handwriting and oil fingered in my hand.

I find my mother's *marginalia* within a book of poems by Shelley.
I find my notes from arrival in Chicago on business as to where
the best restaurants are within five miles of The Ambassador West.
A photo of my other grandfather with a fish from deep in Québec
that looks the size of a bloated horse put through a grape press, and
god knows what it was except that it was big as anything I've seen
and dead as only yellowed paper gets. Another sheet, my father's notes
on meeting with the Goulds, and I expect he knew them better than I
knew the man whose company broke up AT&T, bless you Tom Kelly,
and god forgive me for my belief in your money and your sister and
I'm glad that you were manning the communications lines at Bay of Pigs.
I've got a photograph browned and brittled by 25 years I've found inside my files.

I'm no longer sure what was playing through my head when I placed it there,
or whether I was yearning forward to flesh or away to work when it was
slipped or dropped or discarded or thrown down in anger in those pages
that come up between generations of writers and dreamers and fighters
setting out from home on their own initiative un-owned by any other man

and chasing something that they try to catch on words baited by books growing old and musty on family shelves read once long long time ago. I'm not sure what any of us were doing on any of those long gone days. Hard to find the time to read those words from other generations, but what else is there. Here's a drink to you and you and you, and shadows in the room.

Making Little Things of That Which Is Big

Two days ago at this time
we were walking the dirt road
or more the wagon ruts down
Spencer Mountain slowly
savoring the autumn sun on sage
catching the thrill of mountain rills
cascading over granite boulder
and their gold dried leaves going down.
Slowly, but we stopped to fix the fence
blown apart by wind at the foot of the hill
where the ladies left it latched too loose
before taking the train back to Nebraska.
We scouted the dried red berries grown
so close to the ground they had not been picked
by hikers or even Canadian Jays or squirrels.
nothing. We saw again the abandoned cabin
chock full of rusted wheels and coils and
thought for the first time that perhaps it used
to be part of the old ore mill buildings that
stood there at the turn of the last century.

Not much was said. Not much to say, in fact.
Our flesh was but a membrane of our universe.
Those aster stalks grew by the trail for how long,
and how many aspen trees fell to dust there
before Uncle Sam plotted out the land to sell.
I could go further back as could we all. You will.
On Wall Street the market dipped 240 points.
A soldier at Fort Hood killed 13 comrades.
The clouds came off the plains in long wisps
that came in low cutting off one peak or another.
We talked of things the way men talk of things
when the radio remembers it is connected to radio waves
which are born among the stars and not among commercials.
We make little things of that which is big among us.
We walked down the rutted road and then back up,
and in that alone somehow something was accomplished.

I'm trying to say something without words
about how when you woke without waking
this morning and your legs no longer moved
and your body was shaken with little ripples,
its muscles trying to reach something beyond
that you watched without opening your eyes,
the significance of those mindless gentle and
horrid gestures meant more to me than any dream
we might have had and meant as much across the cosmos
as all we ever had, and somebody had better say it
even among those who speak only with words once,
where words are gossamer things that shift ideas
which have no place or have all place in time and space.

Why Are You Here?

What happens in the spiral of your fingertips
embedded in the flesh you have grown upon bone
formed from the obliteration of novas light years
beyond here coming to this place in space and time...
What happens in the DNA indigenous to you alone
you have left in your lover's body and soul
or whatever else extends beyond your lover that is
unique in the chemical balances the scent the touch
the preverbal lost in the intransigencies of time,
these whorls on the tips of your fingers unique
in all the starburst galaxies of billions of light years
why is it that you have reached out to touch
these things that you embrace in your dreams
with all that you are which is as unique as God
and yet is measureable, is scientifically unique,
is what you alone have carried always as yours
and have held the papers of corporations in
and have worked long hours for a paltry check in
and been abused by the machine of greed. You
leave your fingerprints everywhere on everything
that you love and that you abhor across never
ending eons that started with algae in an ancient sea
and now wash back and forth across a plywood desk.
What happens in the spiraled sworl of time immediate
and in a lifetime what givings and what losings going
where they would if you knew what love was
and the impossibility of autumn leaves burning red
into the fire of generations that are yet to come.

The Reason in Cigarette Butts

The reason is cigarette butts wrapped in twenty dollar bills
is a winter freight train lost in the California deserts
is sixty three birthday cards from hundreds of the dead
stretched across the wireless networks of America. I am
what it butts its head up against time in cardboard boxes.
I am why women's crotches are wrapped in silk panties
when it is raining in Nebraska and the networks sleep.
I am the clouds that bring rain to grass and grass to feed
for no other reason but that the sun has a consciousness
stealing through the infinite miles of black begetting life
that never makes the news or wastes its time on media.
So many years have gone by the reason sits in a chair
rocking back and forth on the porch of a farm in Iowa
ordering pizzas from the Perseid meteor shower, drinking
it all down with whatever comes in the autumn rains.